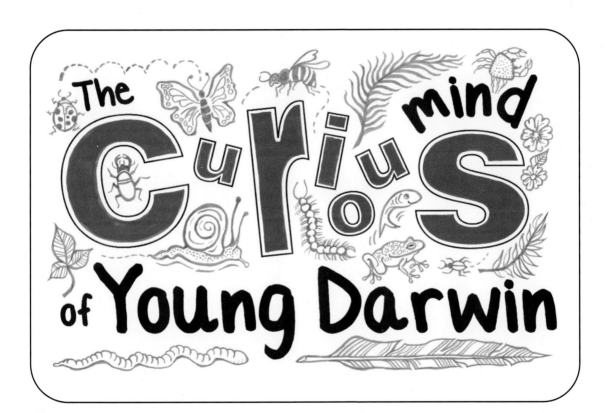

Based on letters and stories from Charles Darwin's childhood.

Written by Sara Bellis, with Caroline Cook and Jenni Taylor.

Designed and illustrated by Lyanne Mitchell.

This edition first published in UK in 2008
by Field Studies Council and
Shrewsbury and Atcham
Borough Council

Text copyright ©
Sara Bellis and Field Studies Council

Illustrations ©
Lyanne Mitchell

ISBN: 978 1 85153 817 1

Field Studies Council
Preston Montford, Shrewsbury
Shropshire SY4 1HW UK
www.field-studies-council.org

Shrewsbury & Atcham
Borough Council
www.shrewsbury.gov.uk

Commissioned and Funded by
Shrewsbury and Atcham Borough Council

www.darwinshrewsbury.org

Part of the Darwin 200 Celebrations

THE CHARLES DARWIN TRUST

*'Understanding natural life and inspiring
a love of science'*

Printed by Cleland Crosbie Limited, Beith, Scotland

This book is not intended to replace
manufacturer's instructions on use of
their tools or chemicals. Always
follow their safety guidelines.

The authors and publishers assume
no responsibility for any injury loss
or damage caused as a
consequence of the use and
application of the contents of this
book.

Parental supervision for activities is
recommended for under 10's.

Hello!

My friends call me 'GAS'. Don't laugh! It's because I do EXPERIMENTS - making big explosions, bright lights and bad smells.

My brother and I have built a laboratory in the back garden. It's all our own space and I love it.

My name is CHARLES DARWIN and this is my scrapbook. It's full of curious adventures and ideas.

Me and my Family

I was born in Shrewsbury and I live just down by the river. My father is the local doctor and we live in a big house, called... The Mount.

Marianne   Caroline   Susan   Catherine

Father

I have four sisters - Caroline, Catherine, Susan and Marianne. They don't usually like adventures.

mother

This is a picture of my mother. She died when I was eight which makes me sad sometimes.

Erasmus

I have one brother, Erasmus. He's older than I am. He's very clever and makes me laugh a lot by putting on silly voices.

I like playing outside with my friends, Garnett, Leighton and Downes.

We always find new places to explore. We build dens, find caves, jump in puddles, catch fish and look for bugs.

My sisters laugh when I come home covered in mud; they wonder what 'EXPLOITS' I've been up to.

They'll never understand that I'm out pretending to fight crocodiles and explore new lands just like my great hero, Humboldt.

Leighton

Downes

Garnett

my Hero

see page 47 to find out more

5

Getting Ready

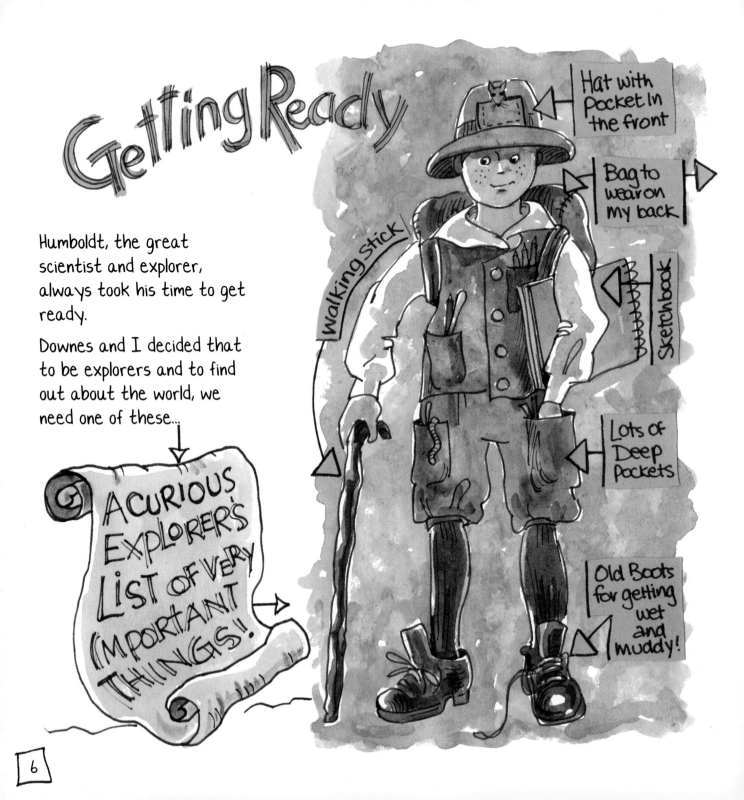

Humboldt, the great scientist and explorer, always took his time to get ready.

Downes and I decided that to be explorers and to find out about the world, we need one of these...

A CURIOUS EXPLORER'S LIST OF VERY IMPORTANT THINGS!!

Hat with pocket in the front

Bag to wear on my back

Walking stick

Sketchbook

Lots of Deep Pockets

Old Boots for getting wet and muddy!

Ball of String (very useful!)

Sketch book

Spoon for digging

My Bag to wear on my back

And of course - Lots and LOTS of boxes, containers, jars and tins. Erasmus says I like collecting things to collect things in!

WARNING!!!

Being an explorer can be dangerous. I always tell an adult where I'm going and when I'll be back. I NEVER do anything that makes me TOO scared.

CHECKLIST:

Collecting pots	
String	Spoon
Walking stick	
Old clothes	
Wellington boots	
Backpack/rucksack	

JamJar

matchbox for tiny things

Plant Pot

margarine tub

Lunch Box for jumpy things

tin Cans

Yoghurt pots for non jumpy things

clear Zip. top plastic bags for flat things

7

I've made a **NET** too!
This is what I used...

An old broom handle (cut off the broom bit!)

Some old wire

An old net curtain

String (told you it was useful!)

Needle and thread

1 Bend the wire into a loop with 2 straight ends

2 → Attach ends to broom handle and tie them...

..on tightly with string. Wrap round and round and round.

3 Fold curtain over wire and sew into place. Sew up bottom of the net.

My net is just like a good friend. It comes EVERYWHERE with me, sometimes even to school!

My net is great as a....

fishing net ✓

butterfly net ✓

insect net ✓

newt catcher ✓

extra bag ✓

hat / flag ✓ ✓

8

I always take a **PAINTBRUSH** with me on my adventures. Here is what I can use my brush for...

1. mud painting

2. gently brushing creatures into pots

So I can look at them without squashing them.

3. Brushing mud off curious stones I find out on my exploits.

4. Brushing a sticky sugar mixture onto leaves and tree trunks then....

...waiting for strange ants and moths to lick it off!

SUGARING

This works best for attracting moths at night.

Ask a grown up to help you gently warm a saucepan full of sickly sweet things. Try using old red wine, treacle and pear drops.

The mixture should have the consistency of milk. Not so sticky that the bugs get stuck!

A MAGNIFYING GLASS My father gave me this old one. I always keep it with me. It helps me look at the tiny details of nature - things that most other people can't see.

A simple MIRROR can turn the world upside down! Hold the mirror on the bridge of your nose and try to walk around using the sky and tops of trees as your guide. I can also look under leaves in search of wild creatures.

A pale coloured BLANKET is useful for catching minibeasts or for lying on to watch the shapes in clouds.

My House

Attic | Attic | Attic | Attic

Head Servant | Store Room | Servants

Stair | Stair

my Bedroom | Nursery | my parents' Bedroom

Father's Surgery | Hallway | Dining Room | Kitchen

◁—Stables | Conservatory—▷

10

These are my BEETLES

All the beetles I've seen have got six legs. This COULD mean that beetles are insects. Look at the different shapes and sizes!

There's so much to look at on a beetle.

This one is a GREEN TIGER BEETLE.

It is bright green and has really long legs which could be for chasing its prey.

Look at his big eyes! I wonder why they are so big?

Isn't it beautiful?

Charles
You must not kill any beautiful creatures for the sake of a collection. There are plenty of dead flies and beetles on your window ledge if only you would clean your room sometimes!

Marianne

I found this in the garden. It's a FROGHOPPER and the young live inside white froth, called cuckoospit.

I've found a dead beetle on my window ledge.
I'd like to add it to my collection.

I soak it in water or alcohol to soften it.

Then I cut a bit of cardboard that's slightly wider and longer than my beetle.

I straighten its legs with the paintbrush, then glue it onto the card.

DATE....... PLACE ....

I've written the date and place I found it on the card and placed the whole thing in a large, shallow box.

I think it would be a good idea to sort my beetles into categories one day, but I wonder how I can sort them? Shape? Size? Colour? Scariness? Ugliness? I don't always look things up in books.
I sometimes like to make up my own categories.

Hmm. I'll think about this in the kitchen and do a little EXPERIMENT while cook is out.

Kitchen Experiment

I poured the oil slowly over the back of a spoon into a glass jar.

It's slimy and sits at the bottom. I wonder what will happen if I make a potion and pour in these other liquids? I wonder what will happen if I use coffee, water, vinegar, cream?

Sometimes it works and I find layers in the glass, a very CURIOUS POTION! Sometimes it doesn't and liquids mix together. The fun is in EXPERIMENTING to find out what each liquid does.

Cook is coming .... QUICK!

I've emptied the cupboards looking for ingredients for my experiment. Here's some oil, milk and treacle...

milk

OIL

Treacle

CHARLES! Are you making a mess in my kitchen again?

Dear Brother,

While you are away visiting friends, I have carried out a most curious experiment in the kitchen. Here is a diagram of my potion (enclosed). Look at all the layers! Some liquids made stripes while others didn't. Can you explain?

GAS

← Oil
← milk
← Treacle

Dear Charles,

You are finding out about density. Density is a way of describing how much matter there is in an object compared to its size. For example, a piece of lead has a greater density than a piece of cork.

Some liquids have higher densities than others, which means they'll sink or float in the glass jar.

Oil has a low density, so it tends to float on water because water has a higher density. Milk has a similar density to water, which means they'll mix together.

Now, be a good boy and you shall have a sugar plum. I'll be home soon and I have plans to do some more experiments in our laboratory.

Your affectionate brother,
Erasmus.

YOU WILL NEED

A paper bag

Two clothes pegs

Some paper tissues

A big splosh of vinegar

Two big spoons of baking soda

A small splosh of warm water

BANG!

Wrap the baking soda in the tissue so that none can leak out. Pour the vinegar into the bag, followed by the warm water. Drop the baking soda package into the mixture. Very quickly fold the top of the bag over twice and seal it with the clothes pegs. Shake and drop the bag and

RUN AWAY!

The bag should expand really quickly, and then explode with a BANG!!!

GAS, you've made a GAS!

The vinegar (really a chemical called acetic acid) made the baking soda (another chemical - sodium bicarbonate) break down and quickly form lots of gas (carbon dioxide). There was too much gas for the bag to hold, so it exploded!

Erasmus.

I am going to make an EXPLOSION!

CHARLES,
Always make sure you follow the instructions VERY CAREFULLY!
Erasmus

I'm going to make a really BAD SMELL!

PONG

smelly rabbit

smelly snowman

← raisins

I can play with the lumps when they are cool. I've made them into curious, smelly shapes.

Heat the milk until warm and add the vinegar.

PHEW! It will smell awful, and the milk will go clear with lumps in it.

HOORAY! A bad smell.

Sieve out the lumps and squeeze them together.

Charles,

Besides making a smell, you have made a solid from a liquid.

The vinegar has made the milk curdle. If you want to make a smelly slime, add some baking soda to the solids and mix them together!

Erasmus

smelly sheep

matchsticks

YOU WILL NEED:	✔
Small saucepan	
A cup of milk	
A teaspoon of vinegar	
A well-aired room!	

smelly snake

I'm going to make a **CLOUD** now.
This is an experiment to do in the dark!

I've Made a Cloud!

ICE TRAY

CLOUD

HOT WATER

YOU WILL NEED:	✔
Heat proof glass container	
A shallow tray	
Ice cubes	
Hot water	
A torch	
A darkened room	

Fill the glass one third with hot water. Place the ice into the tray and put it on top of the glass container.

Turn out the lights and use your own light to see inside the container.

CHARLES
This is how clouds are formed in the sky.

When the ground heats up, water on its surface evaporates (turns to gas) and rises up on a column of warm air ... and cools.

The water then condenses to form a cloud of liquid water droplets.

ERASMUS

Pong

LABORATORY

Keep Out! E.D.

Erasmus is about to carry out a **REALLY DANGEROUS** and **SMELLY EXPERIMENT**.

I can't stand it in there any longer, the smell is too bad. Something with hydrogen sulphide - and it smells like rotting eggs!

I think it's time for another EXPLOIT.

Experiments are great fun!

OPPOSITE PAGE
CAN YOU Find :-

Leighton
Catherine
Downes
Ladybird
Snail
Woodpecker
Butterfly
2 spiders
bumble bee
Squirrel
Slowworm
4 birds ?

my garden

There are probably millions of small creatures in this garden, but how should we get a closer look at them?.... I know.....

LET'S USE THE THINGS IN MY BAG TO HIDE LOTS OF TRAPS AROUND THE GARDEN ⟶

Dig some holes in the ground, deep enough to sink the pots into, so the tops are level with the ground.

The curious minibeasts will run along and fall into a pot. They won't be hurt. We only want to have a close look at them.

Now all we have to do is leave the pots out overnight and see what we've caught in the morning.

But what if it rains? Our minibeasts will drown and my sisters will be very cross with me.

We'll build SMALL COVERS from stones and cardboard so no rain can get in.

Father tells me these are called PITFALL TRAPS.

YOU WILL NEED:	✔
A spoon	
Lots of small pots	
Squares of cardboard	
Stones	

This is the best bit!

What did you catch? I've caught lots, look at these!

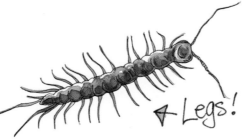

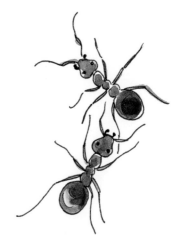

This is a VIOLET GROUND BEETLE.

Look at the jaws! It must eat other animals, which would make it a carnivore!. Look at the colour underneath its body, I'm curious, I wonder why it's that colour?

This is a CENTIPEDE. It is bright orange and has many legs - one pair of legs on each segment of his body. I wonder what it eats?

I've caught a squirming pile of BLACK ANTS. I must have put the trap right on their path! I can see their powerful jaws with my magnifying glass.

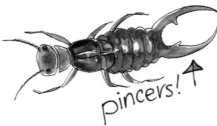

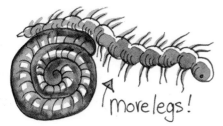

This is called an EARWIG. It has large pincers on its abdomen, I wonder, are those wings on it's back?

This is a MILLIPEDE. It is dark brown and has two pairs of legs on each segment of his body. I brushed it into a pot and gave it some leaves to eat.

When we have finished looking at them, we carefully put them back where we found them. It's fun to watch where they hide.

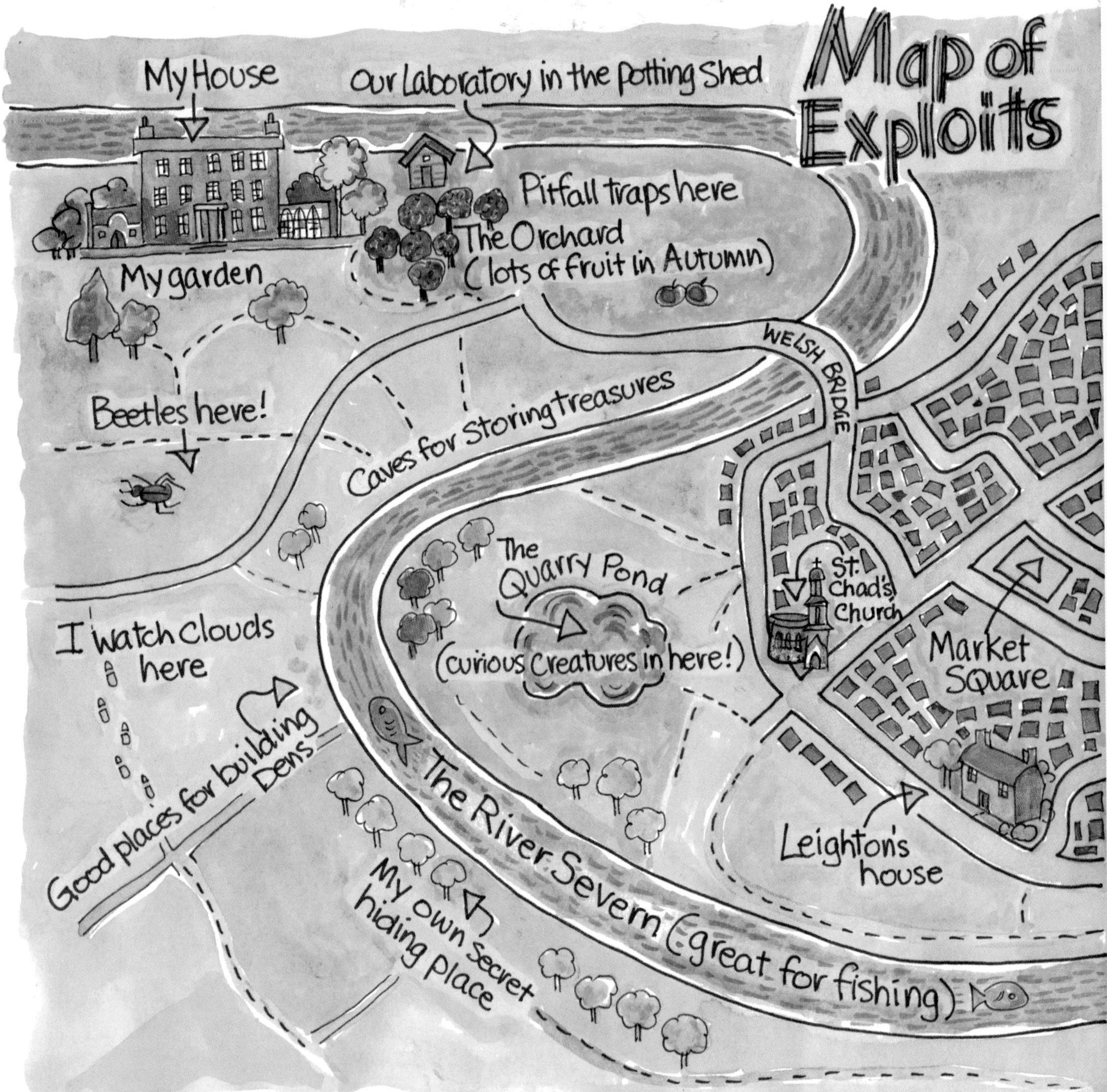

Map of Exploits

My House

Our Laboratory in the potting Shed

Pitfall traps here

The Orchard
(lots of fruit in Autumn)

My garden

Beetles here!

Caves for storing treasures

WELSH BRIDGE

St. Chad's Church

The Quarry Pond
(curious creatures in here!)

Market Square

I watch clouds here

Good places for building Dens

Leighton's house

The River Severn (great for fishing)

My own Secret hiding place

This is the Headmaster Dr. Butler. He is very strict!

My School

The Castle

Strange fossils found here

To Wenlock Edge

The best tree for climbing (Bats live here too!)

The Abbey

To London

Mr. Cotton's Curious Shop

My Church

ENGLISH BRIDGE

Garnett's house (big spiders in here!)

Downes lives here

Owls Hunt here

I'll catch more creatures soon.

NOW I WANT TO LOOK AT SOME OF THE PLANTS IN MY GARDEN.

I like to try and work out the names of a few.

Primrose

It's name means ...
'FIRST ROSE', because it is one of the first flowers to be seen after the cold frosts of winter.

Have a close look at the petals with your magnifying glass... if you think there are five, then look again!

They are all joined together to make only one.

I'm going to press this flower and keep it in my scrapbook.

Arrange the flower to show it at its best. Place it between two pieces of newspaper, then place the whole thing between two heavy books.

Leave it for about a week until it has completely dried out, then stick the flower in a scrapbook.

HERE IT IS, A PRESERVED FLAT FLOWER!

Flower Pressing

YOU WILL NEED:

A flower

Two heavy books

Newspaper

A scrapbook

DIFFERENT PARTS OF A FLOWER

Bees and other insects often visit flowers to drink nectar, a drop of very sweet liquid in the heart of the flower.

Peep into the heart of primroses and you'll find there are two kinds.

In one kind you'll see a little green ball on the end of a stalk. This is called a 'PIN-EYED' primrose. In the other kind, you'll see a bunch of stamens in a ring. This is called a 'THRUM-EYED' primrose.

Erasmus

How curious. I wonder why they are different?

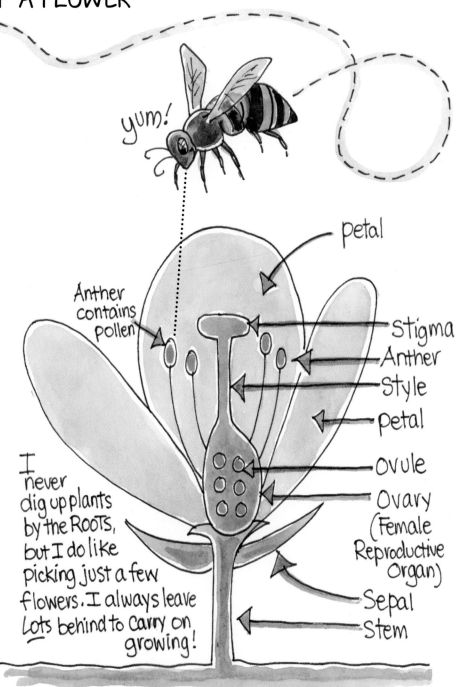

yum!

Anther contains pollen

Petal

Stigma
Anther
Style
Petal
Ovule
Ovary (Female Reproductive Organ)
Sepal
Stem

I never dig up plants by the ROOTS, but I do like picking just a few flowers. I always leave lots behind to carry on growing!

I've told my friends that...

I CAN CHANGE THE COLOUR OF FLOWERS

just by watering them with coloured water!

TRY THIS TRICK......

magic!

YOU WILL NEED:
White flower, such as a carnation
Two glass containers
Water
Red ink (or food colouring)
Blue ink (or food colouring)
Scissors

My mother once explained to me that plants are living things and they need water to drink, so we must water plants to make sure they grow strong.

Take a white carnation, split the stem to about half way up, and place half in water with red ink and half in water with blue ink.

Wait until the next day...
MAGIC!

I'VE CREATED A CURIOUS COLOURFUL FLOWER!

The flower takes up water from the soil through tiny vessels all along its length. The ink stains the vessels through which it passes.

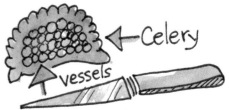

←Celery

vessels

Celery. Cut a slice. You can see the vessels!

I'M OFF NOW TO HAVE ANOTHER EXPLOIT!

THIS IS MY PERFECTLY STRANGE TOOL FOR CATCHING CREATURES HIGH UP IN TREES

Plant pot→

Put the stick through one of the holes

Long Stick

Blanket

This is my father's walking stick and an old plant pot I found in the garden.

I've put the stick through one of the holes in the bottom of the pot and secured it in place.

I can reach up and shake the leaves of a tree with my CURIOUS CREATURE CATCHER.

Not all the creatures fall into the pot. Lots and lots fall on the ground and some even into my hair!

I use the pale blanket to catch the ones that fall on the ground and shake my head to get all the creatures out of my hair! This is what I've found...

green caterpillers
spiders ladybirds
midges snails in trees??
Wasps bees moths

Don't tell Father, but I use this in autumn to take fruit from our orchard. I shake the branches with the CREATURE CATCHER, and the fruit falls in. I can even reach over the high wall when the gate is locked!

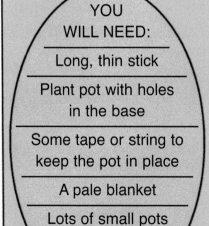

I'll take these apples for cook to make them into an apple crumble- yum!

YOU WILL NEED:
Long, thin stick
Plant pot with holes in the base
Some tape or string to keep the pot in place
A pale blanket
Lots of small pots
A magnifying glass

A Watery Adventure

We should all be back at school soon, but I wanted to explore my favourite place for pond dipping. This pond has got muddy shallows and really deep bits. We use our spoons and nets to catch strange, watery creatures and put them in our pots.

YOU WILL NEED

Home made net (see page 8)
A jam jar
A pale shallow tray
A spoon
Lots of small pots
A magnifying glass

Sweep the net in the shallow water, being careful not to fall in!
Put catches into Jam Jar or tray of water - have a close look with →

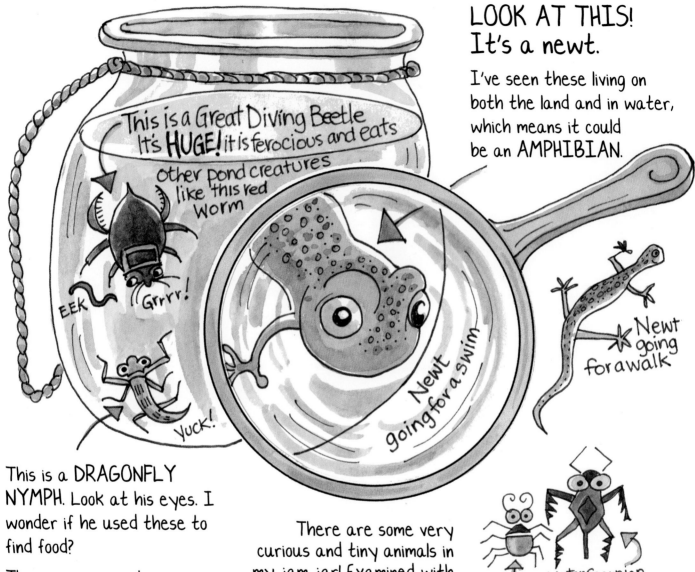

This is a Great Diving Beetle It's **HUGE!** it is ferocious and eats other pond creatures like this red worm

EEK

Grrrr!

Yuck!

LOOK AT THIS!
It's a newt.

I've seen these living on both the land and in water, which means it could be an AMPHIBIAN.

Newt going for a swim

Newt going for a walk

This is a DRAGONFLY NYMPH. Look at his eyes. I wonder if he used these to find food?

This curious nymph swims in a very funny way. It squirts water out of its bottom! One day it will leave the water and become a colourful FLYING insect.

There are some very curious and tiny animals in my jam jar! Examined with my magnifying glass, they look like monsters from another world! I'd have to be very brave if I were shrunk down to their tiny size.

Water Spider

Water Scorpion

Rat Tailed Maggot

Phantom midge larvae

Mr. Cotton's Shop of Curiosities

FISH STREET

Come in Gas!

OPEN

This is old Mr. Cotton outside his shop on Fish Street.

Mr. Cotton LOVES nature. I've drawn a picture of him. He has a wisp of white hair on his head and a huge beard that looks just like a sheep in a rainstorm!

(I think there might be a few beetles hiding in that beard of his!)

HIS SHOP IS FULL OF CURIOUS THINGS!

Glass jars with stoppers, strange yellow pills and potions that make the whole shop smell sickly sweet.

LOOK AT THESE!

He has fossil shells in chalk for a shilling, and gems, rocks and minerals with strange, sometimes difficult names, like sulphur, fools gold, calcite (pronounced cal-site), galena (gal-ee-na), barytes (ba-rite-ees), granite and marble. I cannot imagine a more curious and colourful scene.

Mr. Cotton knows I like collecting gems. He looks out for the new and exciting ones, just for me.

MR. COTTON HAS GIVEN ME A BAG FULL OF STONES AND MINERALS

I will sort them into different piles by finding out more about them.

TEST 1

I held a magnet over the stones to see if any of them were attracted to it.

This one is MAGNETITE and it IS attracted to the magnet!

YOU WILL NEED
A small magnet
A collection of stones or minerals
(A stone may contain many different minerals. For best results, try to obtain pure minerals) We suggest starting with galena, magnetite, haematite, talc, calcite and quartz
A knife (and an adult!)
A magnifying glass
A white unglazed porcelain tile
A copper coin

TEST 2

I can write my initials on a tile using my minerals.

These two grey minerals look similar, but the colours they leave on the tile are very different.

This one is Haematite. It writes with a dark red streak.

This one is Galena. It writes with a grey streak.

TEST 3:

Erasmus helped me scratch the gems with a knife to find how hard and soft they were.

Look at this...

The CALCITE can be scratched with a copper coin, but the quartz can't be scratched even with a sharp knife.

It must be a very HARD mineral!

TEST 4

I have tested the density of minerals in my collection by weighing them.

This one is really HEAVY for its size - it is called GALENA.

This one is really LIGHT, it's called TALC!

I can also sort them into colours, even their smells and their shapes!

I wonder how many other tests I can think of?

Mr. Cotton says there are curious rocks and minerals to be found EVERYWHERE! I wonder where all the stones in my garden came from?

colour

smell

shape

SEASIDE EXPLOITS

We're off on our greatest exploit EVER - an adventure at the seaside!

When we get there, we will be outside every day from dawn until dusk, looking for rocks, crabs, beetles, spiders, strange plants and snakes!

We will have picnics, build dens, make sand castles, go rock-pooling, explore in the sand dunes, play in the sea and collect shells. There's no time to waste,

LET'S GO!

We're down by the harbour, where the fishing boats are moored.

When the tide is out we can play on the sand and collect shells.

LOOK AT THESE!

... mussels, barnacles and limpets.

Their lives must be very hard; one minute covered in salty seawater, the next, high and dry on a sun-baked rock. I wonder why they live where they do?

mussel   Barnacle   Limpet

Here's a space to draw more shells...

LOOK AT THESE STONES...

The crystals in these remind me of sandstones I find at home. This one glitters like gold in the sunshine.

The study of rocks is called geology

skimming stones

I'm going to collect just a few of the really interesting ones, take them home and varnish them for my collection.

my rock collection

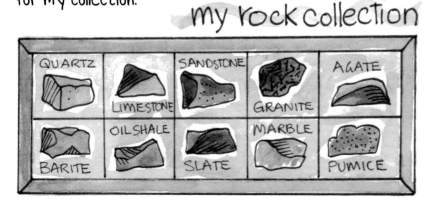

QUARTZ	SANDSTONE	AGATE
LIMESTONE	GRANITE	
BARITE		MARBLE
OILSHALE	SLATE	PUMICE

Sometimes you can find flat round stones for SKIMMING too. I'm going to skim this stone on the sea.

Erasmus says that pebbles on the beach are rounded because the sea has rolled them around and knocked all the sharp corners off them.

HERE'S A ROCK POOL

A tiny crab hiding under that rock... oh, and a beautiful starfish. I'm curious about these barnacles - they seem to be stuck fast to the rock.

I wonder what's holding them there?

There are some very different animals here at the seaside.

I wonder why they are so different to the pond creatures back at home?

What else can **YOU** find at the beach?

Lug worm
Starfish
Sea slug
Sea squirts
Whelks
Barnacles
Brown seaweed
Knotted wrack
Brown shrimp
Mussels
Oysters
Mermaid's purse
Sea urchin
Topshells
Whelks
Sand eels
Crabs
Sponges

WHAT'S THIS? A message in a bottle!

It has strange writing in a language I can't understand. I wonder if it's from someone stranded on a desert island?

I'll write a message back...

Hello! my name is Charles Darwin and I want to be a famous scientist and explorer. I live in England and like collecting beetles. Are you stranded on a desert island? Would you like us to come and rescue you? Please write back to me.
Charles Darwin
Shrewsbury, England.

LOOK AT THIS MAP OF THE WORLD AND THE
OCEAN CURRENTS...

They will carry my bottle somewhere.

I wonder where it will appear?

It's curious to think that we are all part of one huge, CONNECTED WORLD.

I hope my new friend writes back.

We've been BEACH COMBING

and found some things to make a den in the sand dunes.

This driftwood has come from ships wrecked in far off places. They remind me of DINOSAUR BONES, bleached in the sun.

Catherine has used them for the walls. I've got some leaves and dead grass to fill in the gaps of our hideaway.

Here's an old flag lying on the beach. It's a perfect finishing touch. It's big enough for us all to get inside. I'm going to have my lunch in here everyday of the holiday.

OUR DEN

We LOVE sitting in this den. It feels like we're part of nature.

If we sit quietly and for long enough, we hear things that grown ups are too busy to hear. Sounds of birds' wings and rustling bushes, as if nature no longer minds us being here.

It's great sitting low on the ground too. We can get very small and see into the bushes where the wrens and redstarts live.

Was that a SNAKE?

I hope so. I LOVE snakes.

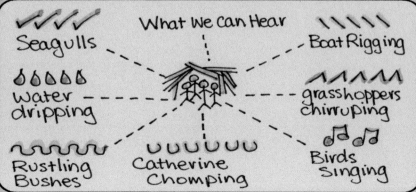

What We Can Hear

Seagulls

Boat Rigging

Water dripping

grasshoppers chirruping

Rustling Bushes

Catherine Chomping

Birds Singing

OW! WHAT WAS THAT?

Something just bounced off my head! It's a very large GRASSHOPPER, look at those big legs for jumping.

But not fast enough to get away from me.

GOT YOU!

Here's a picture of my grasshopper.

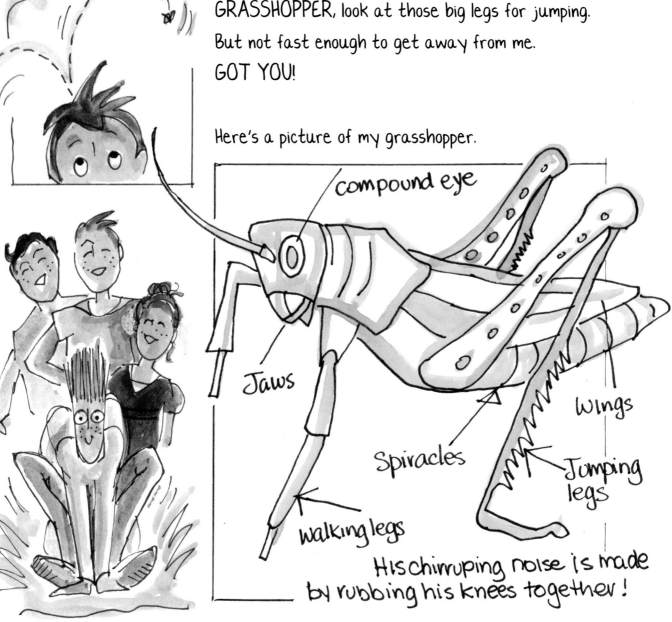

compound eye

Jaws

Spiracles

Wings

Jumping legs

walking legs

His chirruping noise is made by rubbing his knees together!

CURIOSITY is a WONDERFUL thing.

The more we watch, listen and learn, the more the world is opened up to us. I hope this holiday never ends. Friends, a den, freedom and sunny days. What could be better than this?

I will never stop being curious. I have a feeling there is a lot more out there for me to discover.

WHAT WILL I DO TOMORROW?

I made this scrapbook back in 1821. Little did I know then that just a few years later I would be on board a ship called HMS Beagle, bound on a five-year round the world voyage to explore new lands.

This trip changed my life forever.

I collected plants and animals and studied rocks and minerals. I kept a diary of all my exploits, just like my hero, Humboldt.

When I came home, I realised I had seen and collected clues about interesting patterns in nature: birds, flowers, tortoise shells and rocks from volcanoes. I carried out experiments for many years and worked out one BIG connection between these clues. My idea was that species of plants and animals sometimes change over very long periods of time from one generation to another.

I named my idea **"The Theory of Evolution"**, and it changed the way many people thought about the world.

I am an old man now and prefer to have a quiet life, with my wife and children, here at Down House in Kent.

I still do experiments of course! Tomorrow, my son and I plan to collect hundreds of worms and play the bassoon to them. Even in my old age, I *still* have that **curious mind** I had as a child.

Curiosity is a wonderful thing.

Glossary

Alexander von Humboldt (1769 – 1859).
He was a German naturalist and explorer.

His travels through Latin America were famous and Darwin took a copy of Humboldt's travels with him on the Beagle.

Darwin's thoughts on Humboldt:

"He was the greatest travelling scientist who ever lived."

"I have always admired him; now I worship him."

Abdomen – the end section of an insect. The abdomen often contains the insect's heart.

Acetic Acid – a natural acid that is associated with vinegar. Acetic acid is also found in apples, oranges, peaches, coffee and strawberries.

Amphibian – a cold-blooded animal that spends part of its life on land, and part in water. Frogs, toads and newts are amphibians.

Antenna/Antennae – also known as "feelers". They are long thin organs on the top of an insect's head.

Carbon Dioxide – a naturally occurring gas that has no colour or smell.

Carnivore – an animal that eats meat.

Condense – the process of a gas turning into a liquid.

Crystal – a piece of a mineral. Crystals are shapes made from a repeated chemical structure.

Curiosity – the love of finding things, asking questions about them, thinking of ways to answer the questions, then working out the answers.

Experiment – the testing of an idea.

Exploit – a brave deed or adventure.

Exploration – a search in order to discover new things.

Explosion – a big bang! It is often caused by the sudden increase in energy or volume of gas.

Gas – a collection of matter without definite shape or form.

Gem – a precious stone, often polished and used in jewellery.

Head – the segments at the top of the body, containing mouthparts, a brain and a face.

Herbivore – an animal that only eats plants.

Hydrogen sulphide – a poisonous gas that smells of rotten eggs.

Laboratory – a place containing equipment for experiments.

Liquid – a state of matter that has a loose shape, with a tendency to flow.

Mineral – a natural substance that is not a plant or an animal. Minerals have a definite shape and contain crystals.

Oxygen – a gas without colour or smell. It makes up about 20% of the Earth's atmosphere.

Pollen – a fine yellow dust produced by the male part of a flower that fertilises flowers of the same species.

Predator – an animal that lives by hunting and eating other animals.

Reaction – a process in which a substance (or substances) is changed into one or more new substances.

Scientist – a person who observes and experiments to learn about the world.

Segment – another name for a section of something.

Solid – matter that has a definite shape and does not flow.

Thorax – the middle segments of an insect. The thorax often contains the legs and powerful muscles attached to wings.

Mr. Darwin wants to know if we can hear music or just feel vibrations!

Space for notes and drawings...